GREEN ARE GOOD FOR YOU by TONI GOFFE

ACID RAIN! FAST FOODS YEAH! EXPLOITATION OF THE RAINFORESTS!...

First published in Great Britain by
Pendulum Gallery Press
56 Ackender Road, Alton, Hants GU34 1JS

© *TONI GOFFE 1990*

GREENS ARE GOOD FOR YOU
ISBN 0-948912-13-8

PRINTED IN GREAT BRITAIN BY
UNWIN BROTHERS LTD, OLD WOKING, SURREY

WE ARE ALL BECOMING ALARMINGLY
AWARE OF THE DAMAGE WE ARE
INFLICTING ON OUR PLANET.
    SOMETIMES, IT SEEMS, THAT
IT'S ALL TOO LATE TO DO ANYTHING
ABOUT IT.
    YET THERE IS STILL TIME.
EACH ONE OF US CAN DO SOMETHING,
HOWEVER SMALL IT MAY SEEM,
TOWARDS RESTORING THE EARTHS
NATURAL BALANCE.
    HERE, IN THIS BOOK, ARE SIXTY
THINGS YOU CAN DO, THAT COULD
POINT YOU IN THE RIGHT DIRECTION.
    TOGETHER WITH SOME EXPLAN-
-ATIONS OF 'GREEN' TERMS ......

THE GREENHOUSE EFFECT: IS THE WARMING OF THE ATMOSPHERE AROUND THE EARTH; BY THE BUILD-UP OF GASES MAKING THE EARTH A HOTTER PLACE TO BE IN.

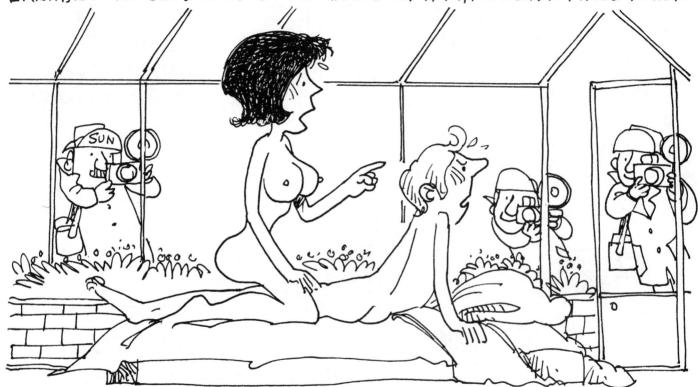

'IS THIS THE GREENHOUSE EFFECT OR THE EFFECT OF HAVING A GREENHOUSE ...?'

TAKE A SHOWER RATHER THAN A BATH — IT USES ABOUT
FIVE TIMES LESS WATER .....

' WELL, THIS IS MORE FUN THAN FIVE LONELY
SHOWERS, ISN'T IT? '

CAR-SHARE WHENEVER IT IS POSSIBLE — IT SAVES PETROL
AND IS A WAY OF MEETING PEOPLE OF LIKE MINDS...

' WHY DIDN'T WE THINK OF THIS BEFORE ?!!?.!.

HAVE YOUR HEATING SYSTEMS SERVICED REGULARLY TO
MAINTAIN EFFICIENCY.....

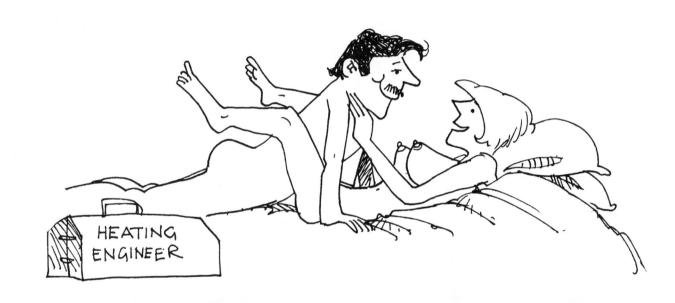

' WELL, I'VE HEARD SOME EXCUSES IN MY TIME.....'

HELP SAVE THE RAINFORESTS — BY NOT USING TROPICAL HARDWOODS IN YOUR HOME .....

LAG YOUR LOFT PROPERLY TO IMPROVE THE INSULATION — IT WILL ALSO SAVE ON YOUR ELECTRIC BILLS.

' I'VE HAD TO LAG THE WIFE, SHE KEEPS TURNING UP THE HEATING..... '

TAKE UP BICYCLING — THE BEST TRANSPORT MACHINE FOR THE ENVIRONMENT AND YOUR HEALTH!!

WHEN YOUR FAMILY NEXT GO ON AN OUTING, TRY WALKING....

THE NEXT FRIDGE YOU BUY, MAKE SURE IT'S A REDUCED CFC MODEL...

' YES SIR, GREATLY REDUCED CFCs. ESPECIALLY NOW AS THE BOTTOM'S JUST FALLEN OUT!'

PACKAGING IS ONLY RECYCLABLE IF YOU HAVE THE
APPROPRIATE FACILITIES OR BANKS NEARBY.....

'DOESN'T IT DEFEAT THE OBJECT IF WE HAVE TO
DRIVE 10 MILES TO THE COLLECTION POINT.....'

REDUCE YOUR SPEED WHEN DRIVING — YOU'LL FIND YOU USE LESS PETROL.

'WELL, YOU'LL BE SAVING A LOT OF PETROL FOR THE NEXT FIVE YEARS WHERE YOU'RE GOING, SUNSHINE!'

SAVE BOTTLES AND GLASS CONTAINERS OF ALL KINDS AND TAKE THEM TO A BOTTLE BANK.....

'WE'VE GOT SO MANY BOTTLES AT HOME, WE THOUGHT THIS MADE MORE SENSE.....'

RAGS AND ALUMINIUM CAN BE RECYCLED TOO.....

WHENEVER POSSIBLE WALK, CYCLE OR USE PUBLIC TRANSPORT ———— IT'S SAFER !!.....

TAKE YOUR LITTER HOME WITH YOU...

'THAT LOOKED LIKE THE FARMER OF THE FARM WHERE
WE HAD OUR PICNIC....'

COLLECT YOUR NEWSPAPERS, TIE THEM INTO NEAT PARCELS
READY FOR YOUR RECYCLING COLLECTION POINT.....

' JUST A SIMPLE PARCEL WOULD DO MA! '

TAKE PURCHASES HOME IN A CARDBOARD BOX: THIS CAN BE USED LATER TO STORE PAPER FOR RECYCLING......

'ANOTHER BOX!! I SUPPOSE YOU WANT ME TO GO OUT AND FIND ENOUGH PAPER TO FILL IT AGAIN EH??'

DRAUGHT-PROOF ALL DOORS AND WINDOWS.....

'I THINK IT'S <u>JUST</u> DRAUGHTS WE EXCLUDE ISNT IT?'

BLOCK OFF UNUSED CHIMNEYS AND INSTALL VENTS
TO PREVENT CONDENSATION.....

'A VENT IS A HOLE IN THE WALL THAT LETS
IN AIR, RIGHT?'

DEFROST THE REFRIGERATOR REGULARLY — IT REDUCES
RUNNING COSTS.....

'I DON'T CARE HOW MUCH MONEY WE'RE SAVING,
WILL YOU STOP DOING THIS....'

ALWAYS TAKE A SHOPPING BASKET WITH YOU WHEN YOU
GO SHOPPING.....

' I THOUGHT YOU WERE JUST GOING OUT TO
BUY SOME VEGETABLES.....'

ONLY BUY 'ENVIRONMENTLY-FRIENDLY' PRODUCTS. MUCH SAFER FOR THE PLANET.

RAINFOREST: OFTEN CALLED 'JUNGLE' AND GROWING ON VERY
POOR SOILS. IF DESTROYED, MAY LEAVE ONLY
DESERT BEHIND.....

'TARZAN, WHERE HAVE YOU BEEN? THIS IS ALL THAT'S
LEFT OF OUR JUNGLE TREE-HOUSE!.....'

DON'T THROW OLD CLOTHES AWAY · GIVE THEM TO SOMEONE WHO MIGHT BEABLE TO REUSE THEM.....

'JEREMY, I DON'T CARE THAT THIS FASHION MAY COME BACK ONE DAY — I DON'T WANT THEM ....'

POLLUTION: SOMETHING THAT IS FILTHY, DIRTY, FOUL AND SMELLY SOMEWHERE THAT WE DO NOT THINK IT IS DESIRABLE ....

'HE SAYS HE'S YOUR BROTHER, AND HE'S HERE FOR A LOAN .....'

FAST-FOOD WASTE CARTONS CAN BE AN ANNOYING FORM OF URBAN POLLUTION — THEY SHOULD BE PUT INTO WASTE-BINS FOR RECYCLING......

'YES, THIS WAS YOUR PARTICULAR PIECE OF URBAN POLLUTION I WAS TELLING YOU ABOUT — WHY??'

DON'T THROW ANYTHING AWAY UNTIL YOU'RE SURE NOBODY NEARBY CAN FIND A GOOD USE FOR IT!.....

'.....AND GOOD RIDDANCE..!

ONLY USE DUSTBIN LINERS WHICH ARE MADE OF
BIODEGRADABLE PLASTIC......

A SUBSTANCE IS BIODEGRADABLE IF IT CAN BE BROKEN DOWN
BY BACTERIA AND OTHER BIOLOGICAL MEANS INTO CARBON
DIOXIDE AND WATER...

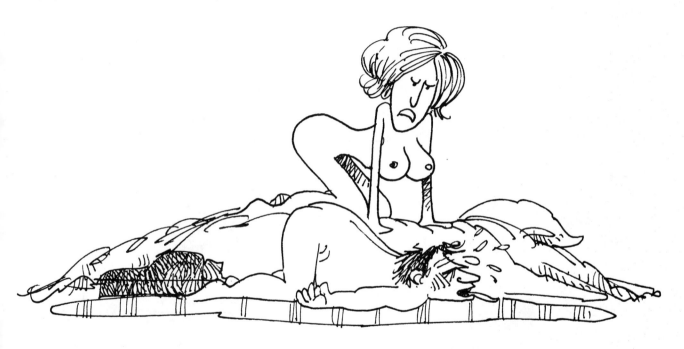

'YOU'RE NOT MUCH USE REALLY ARE YOU ?—
HUMM — I WONDER IF YOU'RE BIODEGRADABLE ?...'

SELECT CRUELTY-FREE COSMETICS AND TOILETRIES......

'... AND WHAT MAKES YOU THINK THESE AREN'T CRUELTY-FREE?'

ECOLOGY — THE STUDY OF THE INTERACTIONS BETWEEN LIVING ORGANISMS AND THEIR EN-VIRONMENT.....

ENERGY FROM SOURCES WHICH WILL NOT RUN OUT ARE SOMETIMES POWERED BY THE SUN.....

'WOW! I THINK I'VE DISCOVERED RENEWABLE ENERGY.....'

'THE ONLY THING DOWN HERE THAT'S GREEN IS — MOULD !!'